PER
MY
LAST
EMAIL...

PER MY LAST EMAIL...

Witty, Wicked, and Wonderfully Weird Workplace Words and Phrases

STEPHANIE K. WRIGHT

Andrews McMeel
PUBLISHING®

Words. They are everywhere.

Two hundred and seventy-three thousand words populate the English language. Delightful words like *fribble* and *borborygmus*. Funky little words like *tetchy* and *quanked*. And gloriously pungent words like *zounderkite* and *smellfungus*.

And yet, we all seem to be at a loss for words. Quality words, that is. We are talking ourselves senseless on social media. Barely listening to each other drone on and on in endless meetings. And glossing over tediously repetitive emails. We just keep spitting out the same fistful of stale words over and over and over . . . and over. Especially at work.

But there's hope. This book will help you become the master of inventive autoreply emails. Help you find lively alternatives for "looking forward" or "my plate is full." Provide twenty new words to snark at your coworkers or if you're feeling magnanimous there are almost as many compliments. Calling in sick? There's a collection of obscure words to explain how you feel. How about a passel of new words to help you simply say, "No"?

Let us answer the call to put some heart back into our words. To strike down dead metaphors and laugh in the face of frazzled phrases. To bend vocabulary to our every whim.

Turn the page. It's time to sparkle like the shiny ball of clever that you are.

PER MY LAST EMAIL DISCLAIMER:

No words were harmed in the making of this book. There have been no amputations, no alterations, no fabrications, and certainly no portmanteaus like *staycation* or *flustrated*. All words in this book are real and exist in one legitimate dictionary or another. Many were found in the dark recesses of dusty books and had to be patiently coaxed back into the sunlight.

Any relation to words created from a secret language you made up as a kid is purely coincidental.

THIS IS YOUR APERÇU

ℓℓℓℓℓℓ

Care for a glimpse into the soul of this tiny world of wonderous words?

This section was named an aperçu to pique your interest. Because, frankly, who reads a "Table of Contents" anymore? In fact, you've probably skipped over it and already memorized five new words for calling in sick.

But just in case your eyes are still traveling down this sentence, do enjoy the spoilers ahead.

ARE WE CONVOKING AGAIN?

Sneaky ways to coax your coworkers into attending what might possibly be a more effective meeting than most. Hey, one can dream.

- Your Daily 10:00 a.m. Black Hole

- You Are Cordially Not Invited

A BRAVE NEW WORLD

How a few keen words can get you out of any video-conferencing scrape.

- I Was on Mute: Navigating the World of Video Conferencing

- Is It Cold in Here, or Is It Just Me? Frozen Again

- What Was That Again? How to Avoid Sounding Absolutely and Utterly Confused

BEING A GOOD NEIGHBOR

Refreshing ways to connect with your coworkers.

- Why Hello There! Entertaining Hallway Howdys

- More Than Fine: Upending the Formulaic One-Word Response to "How Are You?"

LIFE IN WORKVILLE

Because reality.

- Losing Your Mind: Feeling Frazzled Never Sounded so Clever

- Bees & Beavers: Never Not Busy

- Whinging On: A Most Excellent Coping Mechanism

JUST. NOT. FEELING. IT.

Fresh ways to call in "sick" or express dwall. You know, for a friend . . .

- Personal Days: A Little Piece of Heaven

- My Soul Mate Is a Sloth

A BLUE STREAK

Mostly clever ways to swear out loud at work.

ABOUT THOSE EMAILS . . .

You, too, can turn expected, stale email phrases and autoreplies into slightly more interesting offerings that are still, sadly, work appropriate.

- Greetings!

- Goodbyes

- Looking Forward

- Fun with Autoreply

NOT A PEOPLE PERSON

Sometimes folks need a good talking to.

- Tick Tock, People

- Let's Play the Quiet Game

- On. My. Last. Nerve.

OKAY, MAYBE I'M A SOME-PEOPLE KIND OF PEOPLE PERSON

And sometimes, folks deserve a little extra love.

- Hardworking
- Gold Star for You
- I Do Like You

POWERFUL STUFF

Words that help get you what you want.

- Use Your Outside Voice
- Just Say No: It's a Beautiful Thing
- I'm Out: Resigning with Panache

SOMEONE CALL HR

Because, c'mon, you know this crap is wildly inappropriate.

SNEEZING WITH YOUR EYES OPEN

It's not possible to do the impossible. No matter what that inspirational poster hanging in HR claims.

RETIREMENT PARTY

Are you showing your age? Let's just freshen up your vocabulary.

ARE WE CONVOKING AGAIN?!

lllll

Meetings. The Corporate World's answer to the Old World's pits of despair.

YOUR DAILY 10:00 A.M. BLACK HOLE

Meetings are the megalithic time sucks of the work world. Many are unnecessary and most are absurdly long. But since you can't get out of them—how about making the scheduling of them a tad more entertaining?

Constellate

form or cause to form into a cluster or group; gather together

"People of marketing! It is time to *constellate* to interview brand mascots!"

Muster

assemble, especially for inspection or in preparation for battle

"Has the writing team *mustered*, or are they still hovering over their morning coffee?"

Congregate

gather into a crowd or mass

"All department heads, it's time to *congregate* in Conference Room C for the quarterly budget review. Stale croissants will be paired with an equally stale PowerPoint presentation."

Convene

come or bring together for a meeting or activity

"Let's all *convene* in Kevin's office at 12:30 p.m. to rant about the ludicrous new kitchen cleaning policy. Bring lunch—and an attitude."

Convoke

call together; summon to meet or assemble

"Last week, the legal team *convoked* to discuss our next steps in resolving the Ward lawsuit. We will be *convoking* in ten minutes to follow up on those action items. And to eat pizza. We're going to need lots of pizza."

Assemble

to gather people, other living creatures, or objects together in one particular place; yep, just like the Avengers

"Colleagues, *assemble*!"

Foregather

assemble or gather together

"Kim, please work to *foregather* Team Possible to review the new language manuals."

Summon

order someone to be present; for those days when you are feeling particularly imperious

"The entire office has been *summoned* to the auditorium to meet our new mascot, Wonder Cat. See you in five!"

Getred

the state of being together; an assembling of people or animals

"You are invited to next Wednesday's mandatory *getred* where we will be reviewing new office protocols. Bring your patience."

Klatch or Klatsch

a casual gathering of people, especially for refreshments and informal conversation (sounds rather pleasant, doesn't it?)

"Come join us for a brown bag lunch *klatch* today to run through the new video edits."

Coterie

a close-knit group of people, who share a particular interest, goal, or mission; think Swifties

"Tonight the IT group is hosting this month's sci-fi trivia *coterie* in the main lobby."

Parley

a discussion or conference; the word can also refer to a meeting of enemies under a truce, but let's stick to the first definition

"Who would like to join the *parley* over the new uniform designs?"

Boodle

a crowd of people

"We are pulling together a *boodle* to discuss the next big thing. See you at 3:00 p.m.!"

Galaxy

a large number of famous people gathered together; think the Oscars or the Chelsea Hotel

"Marketing is meeting with a *galaxy* of social influencers, so we're reserving the top floor conference suites for them."

Scrum

a confused crowd of people pressed close together in an effort to get something or speak to someone

"There will be enough unicorn plushies for everyone after the product demonstration. No need to get into a *scrum*."

YOU ARE CORDIALLY NOT INVITED

Looking to make meetings more productive? Or at least less tedious? You could announce that the following eye roll–inducing behaviors are simply not welcome.

Blatherskiting

talking at great length without making much sense

"Heads up! This is a short meeting; *blatherskiting* will not be tolerated. Ahem, Daniel."

Chanking

to eat noisily or greedily; think Cookie Monster

"Mark, you've been *chanking* through those nachos for the last ten minutes. How about you mute your phone?"

Peenging

to complain in a whiny voice

"We will be discussing the university-wide pay freeze at today's meeting. Everyone is in the same boat, so *peenging* isn't going to help anything."

Flummery

meaningless or insincere flattery or conventions

"The new director starts today, and she does not take to *flummery*, so keep your noses clean."

Abulomania

pathological indecisiveness

"Please keep your questions brief and clear. Let's not contribute to the already overwhelming *abulomania* surrounding this process."

Toping

drinking alcohol to excess

"Due to the rampant *toping* and subsequent lawn dart injuries at our last off site, this event will be a dry one. Yes, I'm looking at you R&D."

Kipping

taking a nap; one of life's great pleasures, but maybe not so much an at-work pleasure

"I know this is a four-hour process improvement meeting; however, *kipping* when the lights are turned low is not an option."

Argle-bargle

copious but meaningless talk

"All that guy ever does is *argle-bargle* over the cube wall."

Bloviating

speaking or discussing at length in a pompous or boastful manner

"If John would just cut back on the *bloviating*, he might be invited to Taco Tuesdays or even Wine Wednesdays."

Rodomontade

vainglorious boasting or bragging; pretentious, blustering talk

"If I have to listen to one more minute of Luther's *rodomontade*, I will start banging my head on this desk."

Vaunt

to boast excessively

"Be careful. Michael can *vaunt* about his process improvements for hours and hours."

Loads of other words describe the actions of insufferably long-winded people occupying your realm.

HERE ARE A FEW OF THE BEST:

Blustering
Crowing
Exulting
Gloating
Grandstanding

A BRAVE NEW WORLD

Life is a whirlwind of change. One day you're unhappily ensconced in a cube farm with an ergonomic desk setup and the next you're coordinating teams from your dining room table with your cat and your kids acting as surrogate coworkers. Whether you've been relocated home due to a building-wide HVAC shut down, a global pandemic, or a new corporate directive, it's time to badass your way through this new world order.

I WAS ON MUTE: NAVIGATING THE WORLD OF VIDEO CONFERENCING

Who knew you'd be spending your workdays on video conferences? Reminding people to mute or unmute themselves? Or being concerned over whether or not your picture is going to freeze? Welcome to the world of artless overstepping, unexpected dog barking, quizzical internet issues, and diverting toddler interruptions.

OVERTALKERS STRIKE AGAIN

Everyone's favorite awkward moment on a call. Who stepped on whose sentence? Who starts talking first? How about everyone at the same time? Yeah, that's gonna work. Let's see if a little new vocabulary can settle down that conference call cacophony.

Cacophony

a discordant and meaningless mixture of sounds

"Enough of this *cacophony*. Everyone mute themselves but Xena."

Katzenjammer

loud, confused, and usually inharmonious sound; how parents often feel about their kid's music

"Uh. Okay. Wait a sec. Was it Summer's turn? What? I can't hear anyone over this *katzenjammer*."

Bruit

much noise

"Cease this *bruit*! Eze, please mute everyone so we can find some order here."

Ruckus

a state or situation in which many people are angry or upset; picture the returns line at a superstore during the holidays

"All right, all right, everyone slow down. This feels like nothing but a *ruckus* right now."

Donnybrook

a rough and often noisy fight usually involving a bunch of people

"If I didn't know better, I'd say we were in the middle of a *donnybrook*, not an IT call."

Dissonance

inharmonious or harsh sound

"Jen, Ben, and Zev are stepping on each other's sentences, and it all sounds like utter *dissonance* to me."

Din

a loud, confused noise; noisy clamor

"Hey gang, I can't hear any of you over the *din* of all your competing voices."

THE SILENT TREATMENT

Nothing slows down a meeting faster than a clumsy on/off mute situation. And while the mute button can be a glorious thing, work does need to be accomplished. So how about you help a serial-muting coworker out and let them know they are muted . . . yet again.

Taciturn

reserved or uncommunicative in speech; saying little

"Jesse, are you being *taciturn*, or are you still on mute?"

Pantomime

the art or technique of conveying emotions and actions by gestures without speech

"This meeting just improved—Marcel is *pantomiming* his accounting summary."

Mum

silent

"Well, we'd love to hear that theory, Jackson. But I think you've gone *mum*."

Silence is not golden

silence is golden—except the opposite

"*Silence is not golden* in a brainstorming session, people. Unmute yourselves, already."

On the quiet

secretly

"Group Hexagon, I think you're answering that question *on the quiet*."

IS IT COLD IN HERE, OR IS IT JUST ME? FROZEN ONCE AGAIN

You're stuck in time and space. Your colleague is trapped mid-speech by the ethernet gods. Frozen. It happens in every meeting. How many times have you found yourself shouting, "You're frozen!" into your laptop? Tired of channeling your inner Elsa? Try out a few of these stop motion descriptors.

Lapidifies

turns to stone; think Medusa

"It seems this meeting is plagued by internet issues. If anyone else *lapidifies*, we are going to cut off the call."

Glaciate

to become frozen or covered with ice or glaciers

"Argh! Cleo is *glaciated* again! Can someone call IT?"

Gelid

icy, extremely cold

"If I go all *gelid*, just finish the conversation. I'll catch up later."

Algid

cold, chilly; freezing, frozen; frigid; all the wintery things

"I was *algid* for the first half of the meeting. Can you go over the high points with me?"

Rimy

covered in frost

"I'm just waiting for your video to stop being *rimy* so you can finish your thought."

Congeal

to solidify something by lowering the temperature

"Looks like Gladys *congealed* on us."

Static

characterized by a fixed or stationary condition; in other words, motionless

"Let's reschedule this call, as the Colorado team keeps going *static*."

WHAT WAS THAT AGAIN? HOW TO AVOID SOUNDING ABSOLUTELY AND UTTERLY CONFUSED

Your phone won't stop chirping at you during the all-staff meeting. Perhaps your head is still reeling from the tedium of that last call. Or maybe your family explodes with needs during the team webinar. Any way you look at it, your attention isn't on the task at hand, and that's just when you get called on for a response. Now what? Try flinging one of these words around to help spin those awkward moments in your favor.

Shambolic

obviously disorganized or confused

"Pardon me, can you repeat the question? I found the last few slides to be quite *shambolic*."

Gallimaufry

a jumble or confusing group of things; how some people think jazz sounds

"Overall, it seems like there is a *gallimaufry* of decision points for the deadline. Can you explain how you decided on next week?"

Immethodical

haphazard, irregular

"I'd love to make sure I'm responding properly. Can you reframe that last question so it's not so *immethodical*?"

Metagrobolize

to puzzle, mystify, confound

"If the goal of that question was to *metagrobolize* the team, I think it worked. We have no additional comments at this time."

Befuddled

utterly confused or puzzled; deeply perplexed; like watching rugby for the first time

"Well, that diagram *befuddled* me, so if you could walk us through it again, that would help."

Nonplussed

a state of utter perplexity; nope, this often-misused word does not mean calm

"I would ask a few questions, but I'm *nonplussed* by this whole conversation and need more context."

At sixes and sevens

feeling utterly out of sorts, terrifically confused, and overwhelmed

"I missed that last bit. I have been at *sixes and sevens* all day."

All at sea

feeling mentally or emotionally uncertain

"I have nothing to add. I am *all at sea* on this project."

Aprosexia

an abnormal inability to sustain attention

"The speaker was pretty good, but my *aprosexia* won out over her riveting story. I lost the thread about fifteen minutes in."

BEING A GOOD NEIGHBOR

llllll

Five days a week from clock in to clock out, your coworkers are your neighbors, confidantes, pals, coconspirators, competitors, or perhaps even nemeses. Any way those relationships map out, you are in endless contact with them, so why not up your pleasantries game?

Heads up: A few of the hello and goodbye words in this section may be new to you. You'll find them again later in these pages, complete with definitions. However, if you're eager to befriend them right now, feel free to look these fine (and helpfully italicized) words up in the handy-dandy index at the back of this book.

WHY HELLO THERE! ENTERTAINING HALLWAY HOWDYS

Feeling like that stale "Hey there!" and "Mondays, right?" aren't cutting it anymore? How about showing off with a salutation that trips off your tongue.

"What's the buzz?"

"What's the craic?"

"What's kicking, chickens?"

"How goes the day?"

"How farest thou?"

"What's new and exciting?"

"Who's up for a *spiffing* day?"

"Welcome to today, everyone!"

"Here's to another rising and setting of the sun!"

"Salutations, office mates!"

"Happy Monday! Did you shake off the *sonntagsleerungs*?"

"Who's up for a busy day of *fudgeling*?"

"Who's ready to *futz* the day away?"

MORE THAN FINE: UPENDING THAT FORMULAIC ONE-WORD RESPONSE TO "HOW ARE YOU?"

Your coworker throws a friendly "How are you?" your way and you give them a "Good," "Okay," "Fine." For a little spice, you might throw in a "Hanging in there!" or "Glad it's Friday." Ugh. No one is as banal as all that sounds. We can easily do so much better. Let's pop that friendly banter up a few notches, shall we? Perhaps bring some levity to a coworker's day. Or, on the flip side, give yourself some much-needed space.

Feeling like life is on your side? Try these beauties:

Chirky

a late nineteenth-century word for cheerful

"I've had my coffee, met my deadline, and am wearing my favorite shirt. All in all, I am *chirky* today."

Stupendous

feeling perfectly marvelous

"I received my promotion today, so I'm feeling utterly *stupendous*."

Chuffed

happy, delighted

"I'm quite *chuffed* about the extra day off this week. How are you?"

Eupeptic

feeling cheerful; it also means having good digestion, so it's a multitasker of a word

"I woke up to a sunshiny sky and couldn't feel more *eupeptic* about the day."

Frabjous

delightful; joyous

"I am flippin' *frabjous*. What a great day!"

Agog

highly excited and ready to go

"I am all *agog* to get this presentation started!"

Canty

being in a good mood or having a good disposition

"I took a nap at lunch and my boss just gave me a compliment. I am nothing but *canty*."

Affable

friendly, cordial, and warmly polite

"Feeling pretty *affable* this morning. Thanks for asking."

Convivial

cheerful

"Loving my life right now, so I'm feeling quite *convivial*."

Blithe

joyous, merry, or happy in disposition

"Downright *blithe*, Peter."

Gladsome

feeling or being delightful

"Well, hello to you! I am feeling *gladsome* this afternoon. It really is a good day."

Chirpy

cheerful, lively and spirited; think slightly buzzed chipmunk

"I guess you could say I'm *chirpy*. Hence the grin."

Jocular

in a joking mood

"This morning finds me quite *jocular*. Want to hear a dad joke?"

Halcyon

calm, peaceful

"I am enjoying a rare *halcyon* moment. My phone is quiet, I've finished all my immediate tasks, and my hair looks mighty good today."

Golden

full of happiness, prosperity, or vigor

"I am *golden*, Gale, absolutely *golden*."

Resplendent

shining brilliantly; gleaming; splendid

"Today is a *resplendent* day. Thanks for asking!"

Copacetic

fine, completely satisfactory; your day may be just ordinary, but at least the word you use to describe it can be interesting

"All is *copacetic*."

Here's a short list of other words that let folks know all is well but there's nothing to actually get excited about.

Ducky

Swell

Nifty

Peachy

Middling

Hunky-dory

Goodish

Not your best day? Have a go at these utterances:

Compunctious

feeling remorse or regret

"It's a *compunctious* kind of day, my friend. Wish I had better news to report."

Chapfallen

cast down in spirit; depressed; feeling downright rotten

"This heavy rain feels like my mood. I am utterly *chapfallen*."

Vexed

irritated; even the definition seems vexed to have to explain itself

"All in all, the day has me *vexed*. But enough about my bad mood. How are you?"

Narked

annoyed or exasperated

"I could not be more *narked* by that accounting memo."

Tetchy

irritable and bad-tempered

"I am *tetchy*. So many things are irritating the hell out of me. Like Legal's use of Post-it Notes. Why are there twenty-five Post-its on a four-page contract? Why?"

Cantankerous

disagreeable, peevish

"I'd stay away from me today. I am *cantankerous*."

Choleric

extremely irritable or easily angered; a good word to keep people at bay

"How am I? Fricking *choleric*. I could just about punch a wall."

Churlish

rude, unfriendly, and unpleasant

"I woke up pretty *churlish* this morning. I better lay low today, so I don't offend anyone."

Sullen

gloomily or resentfully silent; sort of how Mondays tend to feel

"I'm feeling *sullen*. I may just go hide under my desk and sigh heavily for a while."

Bristly

inclined to aggressiveness or anger

"I would say I am all *bristly* today thanks to a lack of sleep and an overloaded inbox."

Querulous

in a complaining kind of mood

"I'm feeling *querulous*, so I suggest you move on unless you want me to get started."

Irascible

very irritable

"Since you asked, I am all kinds of *irascible*. Maybe I'll feel better if I have a snack."

Ratty

easily irritated or annoyed

"I am feeling *ratty*. Just about anything could set me off this afternoon."

Shivviness

the feeling of discomfort that comes from wearing new underwear; it could apply to your actual underwear or another equally pressing life concern

"Well, my day is just a big ball of *shivviness*."

In high dudgeon

feeling angry and offended

"After that snarky comment from Daniel, I am *in high dudgeon* and ready to write a harshly worded email."

Filipendulous

feeling like you are hanging by a thread

"Oh, man, I am *filipendulous*. I flopped during my quarterly review, and I don't know if I'm going to have a job next week."

Contumacious

stubborn as all get-out; rebellious; basically, every two-year-old ever known

"I am going with *contumacious*—because I feel like today is not the day to push me."

LIFE IN WORKVILLE

The fantastical world of drably upholstered
half-walls, incessant coworker pop-bys,
and that lingering smell of microwaved fish.

LOSING YOUR MIND: FEELING FRAZZLED NEVER SOUNDED SO CLEVER

So, you just returned from vacation and your project list is a
mess. Or circumstances have you cohabitating an office with
a loud-talking spouse. It's time to get creative about telling
people you need time to find order in the chaos. How about you
let them know what you're up against?

Catawampus
in disarray or disorder; askew

"Holy crap, my entire to-do list is *catawampus*."

Agley
awry, a mess; like your twentysomething love life

"I can't take lunch today. I have got to clear my inbox—
it's all *agley*."

Whacking

very large

"You have got to be kidding me. I cannot take on that *whacking* project right now."

Elephantine

resembling or characteristic of an elephant, especially in being large, clumsy, or awkward

"Damn, that is one seriously *elephantine* PM system."

Fracas

a noisy, disorderly disturbance or argument; an uproar

"I can't find anything in that folder. It's as if my email got into a *fracas* with itself."

Tourbillion

a whirlwind

"It's already 4:00 p.m.? How did that happen? This day has been a total *tourbillion*."

BONUS EMAIL PHRASING:

Here are a few friendly ways to tell people that patience is a virtue and maybe just to back off, pretty pony please.

"You ever have one of those days where everything seems to be on fire? I'm still brushing the ashes off of my clothes. I'll stamp out the remaining embers over here and check back in with you first thing tomorrow regarding your request."

"Time is a relative thing. And right now it's speeding by me at a breakneck pace. I know this is a priority task, so once I finish up this whacking project, I'll give you a call."

"Due to pandemic conditions radically outside of my control, my home office has been overrun by home daycare today. I need to put a pause on this work until I can extract myself from the fracas."

"I am currently reviewing your request. Once I sort out the agley action list, I'll follow up with a timeline."

"With the office closure this month, it's been a bit of a tourbillion here. I'd like to take a step back and review what items on your list are top priority and what can wait until we settle into our home offices."

"I've been wading through a few hundred emails today and was so glad to see your note in the mix. I'm looking forward to providing you with an answer to your request by EOD tomorrow."

"I've picked up a number of projects for a coworker who has recently moved on to another position, so my workload is a bit catawampus right now. Once my job responsibilities have settled, I'll reach out to you to discuss your idea further."

"I've been juggling projects like a mad clown this quarter. An expert mad clown, obviously. Please expect an update on your project by the end of this week. Thank you."

"I am thrilled to see your program request pop up in the project management system. However, given the plethora of tasks already assigned that week, we will need to bump back your deadline by ten working days."

"Imagine the peaceful feeling you get watching mighty ocean waves roll up onto the beach. Now, imagine standing in those crashing waves doggedly trying to keep your balance. That's where we are right now. I hope that by next week we will once again peacefully arrive back on the shore. Please expect to hear back from me when my feet are firmly planted in the warm sand."

BEES AND BEAVERS: NEVER NOT BUSY

How many irons do you have in the fire? Are you keeping pace with busy bees and beavers? Is your plate full? Speaking of food, how many fish are you frying? Have tragic events happened to you—like being buried, slammed, or tied up?

It's enough to make a sane person crazy. Instead of using those hackneyed truisms to express your state of busyness, how about these fine alternatives?

Inundated

overwhelmed with things or people to be dealt with

"I've been *inundated* with customer calls ever since we released that unicorn plushie with the rainbow defect."

Besieged

to assail or ply, as with requests or demands

"I have no available time to meet today, as I was just *besieged* by the ad agency and their updated deadline requests."

Negotious

very busy; attentive to business

"With the release happening in three days, the entire team is full-on *negotious* right now."

On the hop

bustling around

"Gotta run. My boss has me totally *on the hop* today."

Snowed under

to feel absolutely crushed by a preponderance of work; think avalanche

"I have 312 unread emails to work through. I am completely *snowed under.*"

Rushed off one's feet

to be exceptionally busy

"If Jasmine hadn't been there to help, I would have been absolutely *rushed off my feet.*"

Abuzz

full of or alive with activity, talk, etc.

"Slack is all *abuzz* about the new CEO hire."

Humming

an activity marked by much life, movement, or energy

"The team is *humming* right along and on track to finish the Klondike project on deadline."

BONUS EMAIL PHRASING:

Here are a few fresh ways to let people know
you are on it . . . albeit a bit delayed.

"I've been on the hop all day but will reply thoroughly as soon as my world calms down a bit."

"My current status: Inundated. More soon. Hopefully."

"My current state: Snowed under. Back to you once I dig myself out."

"Thank you for your email. The office is humming at an exceptionally high level of activity this week, so I might be slightly delayed in responding to your inquiry."

"I am currently immersed in another project but will reply thoughtfully to you soon."

"I am hard-pressed for time this week but will review this project on Monday."

"It's good to hear from you in the midst of a very chaotic week. Here are my thoughts on your email."

"I have been utterly besieged with meeting requests this month. But I have found a few time slots when I can give you and the unicorn plushie project my undivided attention."

"I am just catching up on email now as I have been rushed off my feet all week. Perhaps we can meet Tuesday to walk through this new timeline."

"It's been a jam-packed week—continually negotious since early Monday morning. But let's set up a time to talk first thing next week."

WHINGING ON: A MOST EXCELLENT COPING MECHANISM

Your teammate just stepped on your last nerve. Your boss is in micromanagement overdrive. These days, office life has very little private space and video conference calls are even more invasive. So, what's a person to do when they desperately need to whinge, bitch, or grouse? No need to whisper these arcane insults. You can throw a few of them right over the cube wall or type them into your chat chain. They're not likely to cause much offense.

Wallydrag

a feeble or worthless person

"The entire night team is a bunch of *wallydrags*."

Numpty

a flat-out fool

"I'd love my job if my boss wasn't such a *numpty*."

Fribble

to use foolishly or wastefully; also the name of a milkshake from a big old restaurant chain

"Hey Brandon, today is not the day to *fribble* your time away. We need to be productive."

Ultracrepidarian

a person who criticizes, judges, or gives advice outside the area of his or her expertise; if only a sharp side-eye could eradicate them from your space

"Yes, Baxter, I know to reboot my computer before I call tech support, you *ultracrepidarian*."

Froward

a person who is difficult to deal with; there's always one, or three, in every office

"I just don't think I can handle Clarice's *froward* ways this week."

Lurdan

an idle or incompetent person

"Please, please don't put Beau on my team. I already have to work with two *lurdans*."

Quidnunc

a gossipy person

"Man, Kravitz is the ultimate *quidnunc*. I wonder what dirt he has on me?"

Irksome

irritating; annoying behavior

"I'm in such a bad mood that I'm finding myself *irksome*."

Ninnyhammer

a blockhead; a fool or braggart

"Well, Mason just proved himself to be a *ninnyhammer* once again."

Criticaster

a minor or incompetent critic; why is there always one at your high-profile presentations?

"Wanda is in my review group? Damn it. A *criticaster* during the Q&A is not going to be helpful."

Sciolist

a person who talks endlessly on subjects of which they have only superficial knowledge

"Sure, Steve from HR, let's hear more about the technical specifics of the IT update. It's always educational when a *sciolist* weighs in."

Tumorous

arrogant or vainglorious; bombastic; basically, a big talker who has nothing to say

"This *tumorous* keynote speaker is giving me a migraine."

Ditherer

one who is unable to decide; a procrastinator

"She may be slow, but Patrice is no *ditherer*."

Trombenik

a lazy or boastful person

"We are already under-resourced and behind schedule. We do not need one more *trombenik* on this project."

JUST. NOT.
FEELING. IT.

Perhaps you're sick. Or exhausted. Or maybe you're just not having it today. Here's your handy cheat sheet to cover your escape when you just can't today.

PERSONAL DAYS: A LITTLE PIECE OF HEAVEN

If your mood just drags you right back to bed, let the boss know you are taking the day off due to a humdudgeon or other such infirmity.

Humdudgeon

an imaginary illness; the best kind to have

"Seth seems to have developed a pretty nasty case of *humdudgeon*. I wonder if it has anything to do with his new cube mate?"

Borborygmus

a rumbling or gurgling noise in the intestine

"Dear Elim, I am sorry to call in sick on such short notice, but I'm dealing with some next-level *borborygmus* this morning. I'm hoping I'll be fine by tomorrow."

Peely-wally

looking pale and unwell

"I just caught myself in the bathroom mirror, and I am looking pretty *peely-wally*; I think it's time to go home and rest up with my friend Roku."

Wabbit

exhausted and slightly ill

"I know we have a half-day, all-staff Trust Retreat today, but I am quite *wabbit* and won't be able to join in on the fun. Thank you."

Crapulous

hungover; sick or indisposed due to excessive eating or drinking

"I will be in very late today. I am feeling utterly *crapulous* right now."

Apanthropy

a desire to be alone; an aversion to human company—we've all been there

"Today is going to be a personal day for me. I have been overwhelmed by a mad case of *apanthropy*."

Grotty

unwell

"Did anyone else eat the oysters at lunch today? I am suddenly feeling quite *grotty*."

Ergophobia

fear of work

"I have been overtaken by a wave of *ergophobia*. Please do not expect to see me in the office for the rest of the day."

Sonntagsleerung

Sunday-afternoon depression brought on by the impending Monday workday; check out the thousands of memes dedicated to this very topic

"If I'm going to call in all *sonntagsleerung*, now is the time."

Bilious

nauseous

"Looking at my overpacked meeting schedule has me a bit *bilious*."

Qualmish

momentarily faint or sick feeling

"I stood up from my desk and suddenly felt *qualmish* and weak. I'm calling it a day."

Wamble-cropped

having a rumbling stomach; sickly

"I'll be spending today in the bathroom feeling *wamble-cropped*."

Collywobbles

stomach pain or queasiness; intense anxiety or nervousness; the feeling you get during one of those naked-in-public dreams

"I need to take the day off, as I'm experiencing a mean bout of *collywobbles*."

Quanked

overpowered by fatigue

"My weekend with the relatives has left me completely *quanked*."

Uhtceare

lying awake worrying before dawn

"I am going to be in late today due to an extensive bout of *uhtceare*."

Egrote

to feign an illness to avoid work or some such unpleasantness

"It's a perfect day for the beach. Screw it, I'm just going to *egrote* and call in sick."

Ramfeezled

exhausted or overworked

"I just worked a twelve-hour shift. I am simply too *ramfeezled* to come in tomorrow."

Forswunk

utterly worn out from being overworked

"I will not be coming in to work today as I have become *forswunk* and must return to bed."

Zwodder

a dull, drowsy state

"This *zwodder* is nothing to mess with. I am staying home until I can function properly."

MY SOUL MATE IS A SLOTH

Some days it's hard to muster up brilliance—or even be mildly productive. It's more of a check out Instagram puppies, chat about how you'd spend your lottery winnings, or stare at the inspirational quote calendar on your desk kind of day. On those days you feel and act like this . . .

Eye-service

work done only when the boss is watching; busywork

"I'd love to get back to you about those budget numbers today, Janet, but I'm heavily into an *eye-service* project right now."

Fudgel

the act of giving the impression that you are working when indeed you absolutely are not

"I have no meetings today and no pressing deadlines. I am going to *fudgel* my way through the afternoon."

Bootless

pertaining to specific work or actions that are ineffectual; useless

"Filling out these forms is a ridiculously *bootless* task."

Futz

to waste time or busy oneself aimlessly

"I am just going to *futz* around at my desk until the boss comes back from lunch."

Lollygag

to spend time in a lazy or aimless way; an activity best performed on a long summer afternoon

"Who wants to head to the break room for an hour of *lollygagging*?"

Lackadaisical

without interest, energy, or drive

"Today, I am putting my feet up and riding the *lackadaisical* train."

Dwall

dreamy, dazed, or absentminded state; a Monday-morning affliction

"I'm on my third cup of coffee, and I'm still feeling the *dwall*."

Slothful

straight-up lazy

"I'm going to pass on that status meeting, as I am feeling all kinds of *slothful* this morning."

Bone idle

extremely lazy; Friday-night-ordering-in-pizza, TV-bingeing-on-the-couch-all-weekend level lazy

"Kyle, your *bone-idle* approach to preparing for today's check-in was unacceptable."

Otiose

idle; serving no real purpose

"If I sit still long enough, will people just think me *otiose* and leave me be?"

Torpid

mentally or physically inactive; bleh

"If I stare at this screen much longer, I am going to be completely *torpid*."

Lackluster

lacking in vitality, force, or conviction; uninspired

"That was the most *lackluster* unicorn plushie product review I have ever read."

Farctate

the state of having overeaten; bloated, tired; that post-Thanksgiving-dinner feeling

"I am completely *farctate* after today's lunch buffet special."

Clinomania

an excessive desire to lie down or stay in bed

"I have a severe case of Monday *clinomania*."

Enervate

make someone else feel drained of energy; your standard emotional vampire move

"I can't take another policy meeting. That Paul guy from HR absolutely *enervates* me."

BLUE STREAK

Feeling the urge to bang your head against your desk?
How about letting off some steam by uttering a few of these
relatively safe-for-the-office expletives instead.

Pish

nonsense; translates to piss

"Stop talking *pish*, August."

Naff

tasteless and tacky, but can also be used as a substitute for the word f*ck

"Oh, just *naff* off, Veronica!"

Smeg

all-purpose swear word first heard on the sci-fi show Red Dwarf; *best uttered by itself in a moment of frustration*

"*Smeg* it all, Pete. Just *smeg* it all."

Zooterkins

all-purpose swear word from the seventeenth century

"*Zooterkins!* What did you just do to the database?"

Dumfungled

used up, worn out

"That is one *dumfungled* laptop."

Jackwagon

worthless, lazy, moronic, and annoying; could be a person or a thing

"Whoever left the paper tray empty again is a total *jackwagon*."

Swive

a very handy replacement for the word f*ck

"Could you please just *swive* off now?"

Sard

tenth-century version of the f-word

"This is *sarding* ridiculous. I need to go get some air."

Scumber

formally used to describe dog or fox excrement, but perhaps that level of detail isn't needed at the office

"Oh man, this project is total *scumber* work."

Cack

even more excrement

"I don't care how much money it made at the box office. I stand by my opinion. That sequel is absolute *cack*."

Crikey

not actually a swear word, but can certainly be used in a time when you really want to bellow profanities; best used when astonished or surprised

"*Crikey*, Bob! Can you please change out of your bike shorts before the morning meeting?"

What the cuss

this one serves double duty in that it might just get you a laugh or two

"*What the cuss* is going on in here?!"

WTF!

For all those days when you itch to scream
WHAT THE F*CK!!!, try one of these
clever but clean alternatives:

Thunderation!

A variation of "damnation" used in the 1800s. This one is fun to shout while shaking your fist in the air for extra effect.

Bejabbers!

Substitute for "By Jesus!" Because that was once a very foul thing to say. . . . Oh, for simpler days.

Gadsbodikins!

Translates to "God's body." Which apparently was a swear in the 1700s.

By God's bones!

It seems talking about God's body parts used to be a big no-no.

Potzblitz!

A borrowed German exclamation that means "upon my soul."

Consarn it!

A replacement for "damn" when "damn" was a very naughty word.

Bloody oath!

This one just might stop people in their tracks. Use on its own for extra effect. Maybe mumble a bit under your breath after shouting it.

Holy tinsel!

Specifically for the holiday season, of course.

ABOUT THOSE EMAILS . . .

Ever feel like your email inbox is stalking you? Just sitting there, in your computer, breathing heavily and waiting? Waiting until it can unhinge its gaping jaws and swallow you whole? Yeah, no, me neither.

GREETINGS!

"Hello," "Dear," "Good Afternoon." Yawn. . . . Let's set your email afire! Or at least start them off with a bit more punch. These options run the gambit from staid to daring. Choose wisely. . . .

Ahoy,

Salutations,

Good day,

Good morning, fellow worker bees,

It's a bright new day,

Happy shiny Monday,

Let's start the day with a bang,

Hello from the corner office *(well, not quite yet, but soon),*

Hello, it's me again,

Surprise, I'm back!

I bring good tidings from [DEPT NAME],

Greetings from the home office,

Greetings from my side of the building,

Greetings from the [NUMBER] floor,

Greetings from the pit of despair,

Greetings from the grindstone,

Greetings from the slaphappy,

Greeting from the overworked,

Greetings from the enthused,

Greetings from the affably bemused,

Greetings from the cheap seats,

Greeting from the beleaguered,

Greetings from the small but mighty,

I Come in Peace,

Excited to hear what's new?

Excited to hear what's next?

How hops it? *(nineteenth-century slang for "How goes it?")*

What's shaking?

Thrilled it's Friday? Same here!

Here's today's first missive,

Welcome to your next project,

Congratulations on receiving one more email today,

Look at that, another email,

Thrilling news ahead,

Time to close out the day with an update,

Ending your day with one more request,

GOODBYES

If we're going to start emails with some pizazz, let's close them out with a little creativity, too.

You're the bee's knees,

You're a shining star,

You're a pip,

Check You Later,

Vale,

Toodles,

Fare Thee Well,

With Appreciation,

Oh! You made it to the end of my very detailed email. Thank you!

Excited to tackle this project with you,

I promise it's not so bad,

Wishing you a drama-free day,

Wishing you a splendiferous day,

Wishing you a froward-free day,

Here's to a productive day,

Hoping your day is meeting-free,

Here's to an interruption-free day (except for me, of course),

Here's to meeting all of our deadlines today,

Parting is such sweet sorrow,

Keep the faith,

I Shall Return,

May the odds be ever in your favor,

Live Long and Prosper,

To Infinity and Beyond,

There Is No Try, Only Do or Do Not,

LOOKING FORWARD

Some phrases are popular because they are pretty near perfect. "Looking forward to hearing from you" is an email gem. It nicely balances being polite with a sense of urgency. But it has become as ubiquitous as superhero movies. If you are looking to mix it up, give one of these phrases a go:

I am excited to hear your thoughts.

I have every confidence that you will reply soon.

I'm banking on your quick reply.

Hoping to hear from you at your earliest convenience.

I anticipate your thoughtful reply.

I happily await your reply.

Hankering to hear from you soon.

Exuberantly anticipating your thoughts on this matter.

Buoyed by the thought of your speedy reply.

Hope to hear back from you later this week.

I'll count on hearing from you soon.

Counting the minutes until your reply.

Refreshing my inbox eagerly in hopes of hearing from you soon.

Patience is not my strong suit but I'm giving it a go while I anticipate your response.

Curled up under my desk quietly awaiting your reply.

Methodically binge-eating gummy bears while I await your reply.

Inhale, exhale, check my inbox for your reply. And repeat.

Going to check out the latest Twitter drama while you consider my proposal.

Filling my time with TikTok videos while I await your reply.

Watching "work-related" TED Talks while I wait for your response.

Did you know that "floccinaucinihilipilification" is one of the longest words in the English language? I'm going to dig up a few more of these doozies while I await your response.

When you are ready to discuss, you can find me engrossed in Wikipedia's list of conspiracy theories.

FUN WITH AUTOREPLY

Sometimes, announcing you're out of the office for a spell deserves a bit of zing. Here are some creative email options to keep your colleagues informed of your doings.

Hello, I am out of the office creating work/life harmony. I will be off from [DATE to DATE] and will probably be delayed in email responses, but I look forward to harmonizing with you again soon.

Thank you for your patience!

ℓℓℓ

Hello there. I am out of the office until [DATE]. I know that sounds like a long time, but there are people here who have got your back. So, breathe and reach out to [EMAIL] who will have you feeling like "[YOUR NAME] who?" in no time.

ℓℓℓ

I am off traveling the world. I'll be back [DATE], filled with inspiration to jump back into our work together. Plus, I'll bring you back one of those cute little snow globes from the airport gift shop.

ℓℓℓ

The world is a big blue marble, and I'm out exploring it. I'll be out of the office from [DATE to DATE]. Try not to miss me too much. Maybe just a little. But not enough to call. Seriously.

ℓℓℓ

I am out of the office until [DATE] and will not be checking emails in my absence. I know you are working right now while I am sitting on a beach staring at the bluest of oceans, so here's a kitten video to cheer you up.

ℓℓℓ

WOOHOO! I AM ON VACATION!!!! I am off spending too much money, getting sunburned, overindulging on dessert, and loving every minute of it. I'll be back in the office on [DATE].

ℓℓℓ

This autoreply signals that I am not in the office.

Where am I? I could be attending a comic book convention. Or rock climbing in Yosemite. Or at a state fair pie-eating contest. Or out saving sea turtles. Or winning a fortune in Las Vegas. Wherever I am, I'll fill you in on the details when I'm back on [DATE].

ℓℓℓ

This autoreply signals that I am not in the office. And won't be until [DATE]. Try to contain your envy.

ℓℓℓ

This autoreply signals that I am not in the office. I won't be back until [DATE]. Good luck to you.

ℓℓℓ

Definition of Vacation: An extended period of leisure and recreation, especially one spent away from home or in traveling.

I am off doing some much-needed leisuring. While I don't care to think about it while I am recreating, I will be back in the office on [DATE].

ℓℓℓ

Spending a few quality days staycationing with the dog. Much pizza will be consumed, many hours will be spent at the dog park, and more than a few evenings will feature couch snuggling. I'll be back at work on [DATE]. My dog will remain unemployed.

ℓℓℓ

I am out of the office until [DATE]. Until then, please enjoy this photo of me at my desk working hard. It might make missing me a bit easier. Or it could be kind of creepy. Talk soon!

ℓℓℓ

Autoreplies. Ugh. No one likes them, but here we are. I may be out of the office until [DATE], but I can still direct you to someone who can help. Just reach out to [EMAIL] and they will be happy to support you in my absence.

Here it is. The dreaded autoreply. Now what? Your first email may not have gotten you what you need, but I guarantee that [EMAIL] will be able to help you out.

I am out of the office until [DATE]. I will be checking email sporadically (also: intermittently, occasionally, now and then, sparingly, infrequently, and periodically). In other words, not often.

Now that all disclaimers have been met, I wish you a splendid week.

Yeah. It's an autoreply. And yes, I am out of the office until [DATE]. Would you feel better about my absence if I said I was thinking about you and your project? Okay, let's pretend that I am. See? You're feeling better already. See you soon.

You know how everyone says they'll be thinking of you while they are on vacation? Well, I am on vacation until [DATE], and the only thought I'm having is where to explore next. However, my colleague, [NAME], is thinking about you and can be reached at [EMAIL].

lll

Vacation. Holiday. Respite. Work Recess. Email Break. Office Intermission. Productivity Interlude. Any way you look at it, I am out of the office until [DATE]. Wishing you productive, constructive, fruitful, worthwhile workdays while I am gone.

lll

Last week I was stomping out deadline fires. This week I'm hiking in the mountains. Life is funny like that. See you back in the office on [DATE]. Until then, give [EMAIL] a shout for any support you might need.

lll

I know you were expecting a productive reply to your email. However, I am on vacation being anything but productive. I shall return to my usual productive self on [DATE]. Until then, please contact [EMAIL] who will be very happy to help you out.

lll

Did you know that the word "vacation" was first used in *The Canterbury Tales*? Why is that relevant to a work email, you ask? Because I am on vacation. A long, happy, carefree vacation. I'll come down from the clouds and be back at my desk on [DATE].

ℓℓℓ

Hello All! Remember how much fun recess was when we were kids? Well, I am taking a bit of a work recess right now to relax with my family. I'll be back at it on [DATE]. Here's hoping you can find a little of your own recess joy while I'm away.

ℓℓℓ

Hello All! I will be out of the office until [DATE]. To amuse and confound you in my absence, here's a link to Wikipedia's list of conspiracy theories. https://en.wikipedia.org/wiki/List_of_conspiracy_theories

ℓℓℓ

Hello All! I will be out of the office until [DATE]. To amuse you in my absence, here's a link to Wikipedia's list of minor planets named after people. https://en.wikipedia.org/wiki/List_of_minor_planets_named_after_people

ℓℓℓ

Hello All! I will be out of the office until [DATE]. To keep you on your toes in my absence, enjoy this intriguing Wikipedia list of life's common misconceptions. http://en.wikipedia.org/wiki/List_of_common_misconceptions

ℓℓℓ

I am venturing out into the world! I will be out of the office cavorting in the great out of doors until [DATE]. I plan to return to work sunburned, scraped up, and very happy. See you soon.

ℓℓℓ

I am out of the office adventuring. I'll be back at my desk on [DATE]. Until then . . .

"The world's big and I want to have a good look at it before it gets dark." —John Muir

ℓℓℓ

I will be out of the office breathing in fresh air and exploring grand vistas until [DATE]. In my absence, I leave you with this thought: "Wilderness is not a luxury but a necessity of the human spirit." —Edward Abbey

ℓℓℓ

"I haven't been everywhere, but it's on my list." —Susan Sontag

I am currently busy checking places off my list. I will be back in the office on [DATE], refreshed and ready to respond to your email.

NOT A PEOPLE PERSON

≈≈≈≈≈≈

People. Enough said.

TICK TOCK, PEOPLE

Tired of folks spewing nonsense in meetings, all-day workshops, or in what should have been concise reports? Let them know they are wasting your time with all of their codswallop. It's a hearty list because applesauce can be rather prevalent at work.

SUCH NONSENSE

Here's a sleek list of words that all mean speaking or writing nonsense. Use freely on those occasions when you need to call out someone who is blathering in your general direction.

Codswallop

nonsense, whether written or spoken

"The first cut of that video ad is overblown *codswallop*."

Prattle

to talk in a foolish or simpleminded way; babble

"Is Paula still *prattling* on about who's following her on Instagram?"

Malarkey

meaningless talk

"How about you two knock off the *malarkey* and finish working up that report?"

Hokum

out-and-out nonsense; for use when the absurdity reaches hazardous levels

"That email about how Mercury being in retrograde caused you to miss your deadline is pure *hokum*."

Piffle

nonsensical words usually spoken but could be written

"Is it possible for Donald to open his mouth without a load of *piffle* falling out of it?"

Bosh

absurd or foolish talk; like when you say you aren't going to finish that last slice of pizza—please

"You have to admit, Bekah's *bosh* makes for a much more entertaining meeting."

Applesauce

ridiculousness

"So much *applesauce* being tossed around the room and yet so few solutions."

Bilge

nonsense; rubbish

"What a wild load of *bilge*."

Flapdoodle

absurd speech or action

"Steer clear. Finn's *flapdoodle* chatter is in high gear today."

Bunkum

insincere talk

"That press release was overflowing with *bunkum* about the new government policy."

The list of words describing nonsense is long. Here are a few more delightful options:

Balderdash
Tosh
Blither
Claptrap
Fiddle-faddle
Poppycock
Hoodoo
Fudge
Humbuggery
Slush
Tommyrot

LET'S PLAY THE QUIET GAME

Telling someone to shut up is unprofessional and downright rude. You're better than that. But wow, sometimes people need to just . . . let's say shush. Here are a few choice expressions to use with great care.

PUT A PIN IN IT

Hold that idea and we will come back to it later. But will we, really? This tried-and-true phrase is just a business-y way of saying, "Shh." You could also say:

Button it
be quiet

"Let's *button it* for now, Lucas. This isn't your project."

Cut the cackle
stop talking nonsense and get back to work

"Oh my freakin' stars. Can we just *cut the cackle* and review the proofs?"

Save it
stop talking about that project/person/event now; we can talk about it later—maybe

"Please *save it*, Bob. We've all already heard about how much you hate your new cubicle."

Shush
be quiet

"I don't mean to sounds like a stern librarian but man, everyone needs to *shush*."

ON. MY. LAST. NERVE.

Feeling wildly undone? These words may help you regain some sanity. But be forewarned, they are particularly snarky. Use with care. And a good deal of verve.

Scobberlotcher

a phenomenally lazy human

"Janice, you've made absolutely no progress on your quarterly goals. I have never met a *scobberlotcher* of your caliber."

Quisby

a person who actively shies away from anything work-like

"Could that lazy manager be more of a *quisby*?"

Smellfungus

a wet blanket, a killjoy; also a wonderfully amusing word to toss around

"I was having so much fun until our resident *smellfungus* showed up to kill the vibe."

Cumberworld (also Cumberground but never Cumberbatch)

fantastically unproductive, spending time just taking up space

"Today, I am just going to sit at my desk and be a full-blown *cumberworld*."

Snudge

an intentionally mean human being, stingy; think Scrooge pretransformation

"My boss is refusing to take advantage of our freelance budget because he's a *snudge*."

Poltroon

someone who is quite cowardly

"Those *poltroons* upstairs say the right things to the higher-ups but get nothing done."

Berk

an inane, ridiculous human

"I've read the report three times and it still doesn't make sense to me. I feel like an absolute *berk* right now."

Loiter-sack

a seventeenth-century term for a deadbeat, a slouch

"*Loiter-sacks* are a dime a dozen on the third floor."

Gobermouch

a meddlesome, inappropriately curious person; like that coworker who hunts down your dating profiles

"My cubemate is a spectacular *gobermouch*—he's always asking way-too-personal questions."

Gnashgab

a perpetual complainer, a whiner with never a solution to offer

"I don't have time for a venting session today. Keep your *gnashgab* self out of my cube until I'm past this deadline."

Raggabrash

a disorderly or disheveled person

"Just because you worked out at lunch does not mean you should parade around the office all *raggabrash* for the rest of the day."

Roister-doister

a complete blowhard, gasbag, vocal know-it-all

"I cannot handle one more *roister-doister* spewing his grandiose opinions at me today."

Lubberwort

a listless, foggy-headed person

"Colin is an outright *lubberwort* today; I'm waiting on him for ten different things."

Pillock

basically, a fool

"This commute is killing me. The roads are teeming with *pillocks* who can't seem to stop texting while driving."

Zounderkite

a nitwit

"Generally speaking, I am a complete *zounderkite* most mornings. My brain just doesn't kick in until at least lunchtime."

Zoilist

an exceedingly demanding, biting, and hypercritical person

"I want to keep close to the meeting agenda tomorrow. We can't have a *zoilist* like Cheryl taking us off track with unsolicited input."

Snoutband

someone who revels in correcting others in conversation often by speaking over them; like your great-aunt Rose

"That *snoutband* who kept interjecting clearly thought this product rollout was a town hall forum."

Skelpie-limmer

a misbehaving child

"Is Victor still sulking about being taken off the unicorn plushie account? You lost a project, not your job, you big *skelpie-limmer*."

Saddle-goose

a fool

"I feel like a huge *saddle-goose* after blowing that presentation this morning."

OKAY, MAYBE I'M A SOME-PEOPLE KIND OF PEOPLE PERSON

Magic words to dust off when good people do good stuff.

HARDWORKING

There are great people working their butts off around you every day. People who are driven, always on point, and solve the seemingly unsolvable. They deserve a little love. So how about celebrating them with a few choice words?

Diligent

constant in effort to accomplish something; attentive and persistent in doing anything

"You are as *diligent* about replying to urgent emails as you are about your on-point sartorial game."

Industrious

working energetically and devotedly; hardworking

"Your *industrious* work ethic is greatly appreciated by both your team and your clients."

Conscientious

careful and painstaking; meticulous; scrupulous

"Abby's attention to detail makes her the most *conscientious* coder on my team."

Assiduous

showing perseverance; consistent in application or effort; industrious

"Your *assiduous* attention to detail in your reports is so helpful in leading the team to actionable conclusions."

Sedulous

painstakingly diligent in application or attention

"Your *sedulous* craftsmanship helped create our bestselling toy this year."

Unflagging

tireless; persistent; think social media ads

"The *unflagging* determination you've shown in correcting the Q2 rainbow defect errors is impressive."

Indefatigable

incapable of being tired out; unending energy

"Your *indefatigable* enthusiasm about our line of unicorn plushies has made you the only choice for brand ambassador."

GOLD STAR FOR YOU

Let's celebrate great work by outstanding people with descriptors that sparkle. Let everyone know how much those folks shine up the place.

Crackerjack

a person or thing that shows marked ability or excellence

"Charles is one *crackerjack* fitness trainer."

Dabster

someone who is excellent at something

"Dang, Alec, you are an undercover karaoke *dabster.*"

Bosting

very good, excellent

"Evan is a *bosting* carpenter. Let's see if we can poach him for our cat condo skyscraper project."

Prodigious

remarkably or impressively great in extent, size, or degree

"Richard's *prodigious* understanding of space travel has been invaluable as we put together that SpaceX parody."

Consummate

complete or perfect; supremely skilled; superb

"Milena is a *consummate* professional, and that's why she manages all the high-profile accounts."

Veritable

being truly or very much a thing

"MaryDawn is a *veritable* encyclopedia of chicken facts. Let's bring her into the ad copy meeting."

Spiffing

most splendid; like a no-meeting Friday

"Jay's absolutely *spiffing* work creating a Mandalorian-themed event really impressed the C-suite."

Ripping

incredibly good

"Rochelle's whimsical approach to her art show made it a *ripping* success."

Ace

excellent; outstanding

"Once again, Trev's *ace* customer service skills saved our bacon."

Brilliant

having or showing great intelligence, talent, or quality

"Malcolm, your insights on the unicorn market have been bloody *brilliant!*"

Dazzling

to impress deeply; astonish with delight

"Gina's execution of this rollout was *dazzling* to behold."

Superlative

of the highest kind, quality, or order; surpassing all else or others

"Elona's approach to the relaunch was *superlative*; she knocked it out of the park."

I DO LIKE YOU

Pleasantries to bestow upon your fellow cubelings. Because some people deserve a little love—professionally, that is.

Affable

good-natured; a delightful person to chat with

"Who wouldn't want to be as *affable* as Joannie? She makes every meeting a joy."

Amiable

good-natured, friendly

"On my best days I am nowhere near as *amiable* as Kara."

Gregarious

enjoys the company of others; sociable

"Liz is wonderfully welcoming. She's naturally *gregarious*."

Selcouth

strange, rare; unfamiliar; marvelous, wondrous; so many of the good things wrapped into one word

"I'd love to figure out what's going on in your delightfully *selcouth* mind, Serine."

Sprauncy

smart or showy in appearance; fashionable

"Looking mighty *sprauncy* today, Clark."

Beneficent

doing good or causing good to be done; kindly in action or purpose

"Charmaine is the most *beneficent* person in this office. She gave up her Monday meeting donut so our new intern could have one."

Equanimous

even-tempered, balanced

"Ask Heidi to weigh in on that thorny issue. She is always *equanimous*."

Sagacious

wise, discerning

"Thanks for the *sagacious* advice, Schuler."

Micawber

an eternal and unrelenting optimist; in a good way

"We could all benefit from your *micawber* approach to life, Katie."

Deipnosophist

someone skilled at informal chitchat; although this word is anything but informal.

"We need our best *deipnosophist* to take a class of sixth graders on a tour."

Splendiferous

splendid; magnificent; fine

"Your outfit is perfectly *splendiferous*, Carmen."

Impavid

without fear; bold, brave

"You get out there and grab that promotion, my *impavid* friend!"

POWERFUL STUFF

llllll

Words that help you get what you want.

USE YOUR OUTSIDE VOICE

It's time to speak up about that delayed job reclassification, that egregious HR policy, or another project assignment with that astoundingly lackadaisical coworker. Use these stern words to say you have had enough.

Inveigh

to protest strongly or vehemently

"I was guaranteed this raise six months ago, and I must *inveigh* heavily against further delay. Oh yeah, *inveigh*."

Censure

to express severe disapproval of (someone or something), especially in a formal statement

"Due to a high level of tomfoolery, the design team has been formally *censured* and is banned from the coffee lounge for the next two weeks."

Castigate

to reprimand severely

"If you review the egregious actions of the accounting department during last quarter's audit, you will understand why they were *castigated* by the CFO this week."

Remonstrate

to make a forcefully reproachful protest

"The next time you steal my lunch, Matt, I will *remonstrate* you in front of the entire floor. Seriously."

Vituperate

to blame or insult someone in strong or violent language; the backbone of every reality show ever

"I could *vituperate* you right now, Wanda. Go ahead, say one more thing about the already finalized product specs."

JUST SAY NO: IT'S A BEAUTIFUL THING

Oh, you know you want to say it. Again and again. No, I won't take on Sam's overflow work. No, I can't extend your deadline. No, it's not okay to pay my contract late. But how to be diplomatic while shutting that bilge down? Here are some pretty good ideas. Of course, you can always be disinclined to use them.

Disabuse

persuade someone that an idea or belief is mistaken

"I would like to *disabuse* you of the idea that Claire is available to work on your assignment. She is not."

Repudiate

to declare not to be true

"I am going to *repudiate* your claim that I have free time to take on training the interns. I am booked up through the end of the month."

Nix

expressing denial or refusal

"I'm going to *nix* that idea before we all put any more effort into developing it."

Cast a pall

to create an unpleasant situation or mood; like forcing someone to chat before they've had their first cup of coffee

"I hate to *cast a pall* over your planning discussions, but we won't be engaging that contractor after the goblin action figure disaster of '09."

Gainsay

to state that something is untrue or invalid

"I didn't want to *gainsay* you on the call, but those budget cuts are not feasible for the workload we have."

Disincline

adverse or unwilling in action or temperament

"Your lack of data *disinclines* me to grant your request."

I'M OUT: RESIGNING WITH PANACHE

You are positively itching to move on. New job, new you. Right? It's exciting news that needs more than the standard resignation language. Craft a notice that sends you off with a bit of flourish—whether you're looking for a grand exit or a lighthearted farewell.

Relinquish

to withdraw or leave behind

"I hereby *relinquish* my title of Senior Unicorn Engineer and walk out into the world a proud and happy unemployed person."

Renounce

to give up or resign, usually by formal declaration

"As of Friday, I wholeheartedly and unequivocally *renounce* my position as another cog in the wheel of this mega-corporation."

Demit

to resign a job, public office, etc.

"In a happy fit of 'came to my senses,' I have decided to *demit* my position as project manager for the fulfillment center to pursue more sane environs."

Stand down

to leave a job or position, especially an important one; sometimes, standing down is the best way to stand up

"It is clear that senior leadership and I are diametrically opposed on the next steps for the company, so it only makes sense that I *stand down* at this time."

Decamp

to depart quickly, secretly, or unceremoniously

"I met with my financial planner last night and learned that I finally have the wherewithal to open my bed and breakfast. So I am *decamping* and moving to Maine next month."

Bow out

to give up a job, especially when you have had it for a long time

"Today is the day I *bow out* and bid you farewell. Thank you to my colleagues for an exciting work adventure with an incredible organization, but it's time for me to focus on my baking career."

Scarper

to leave a place, often for another

"While you are all brilliant coworkers, I have made the considered decision to *scarper* and head over to Gimbel's to take over their purchasing department."

SOMEONE CALL HR

If you think about it—and really, please don't linger too long or you'll need to wash your brain—these phrases are wildly inappropriate. Anyone uttering them did not pay attention during their mandatory sensitivity training workshop.

Open kimono

To be transparent, to reveal all.
Now think about what image "open kimono" brings up.
Sexist and racist. Best to put this one out to pasture.

Instead, try:

Unambiguous

Conspicuous

Explicit

Forthright

Upfront

Transparent

Transpicuous

Drinking the Kool-Aid

To unthinkingly accept an idea or action.
This is a reference to the tragic 1978 Jonestown massacre.
Whoever utters this phrase is incredibly
unthinking themselves.

Instead, try:

Credulous

Zealot

Lemming

Dupe

Uncritical

Cut your own throat

Bring about your own ruin.
Which you could do to your career
if you use this phrase often enough.

Instead, try:

Self-destructive

Against our own interests

One's own worst enemy

Pernicious

Getting into bed with

To enter into a relationship with someone or something, often, but not always, one that is considered unseemly for some reason. Unseemly, much like using this phrase at work.

Instead, try:

Ally

Collaborate

Conspire

Hobnob

Join forces

SNEEZING WITH YOUR EYES OPEN

Some things are just straight-up impossible. No one can give more than 100 percent. Gorillas never even reach 800 pounds. How about we take these fantastical superlatives down a notch and replace them with accessible words?

GIVING 110 PERCENT

Putting everything into a project. Giving it your all—plus some. Because apparently doing your job really well requires some kind of funky new math. Instead, try:

Persevere
continuing on, even in the face of difficulty or with little or no indication of success

"Annabelle's *perseverance* in learning Swedish is paying off. She can already translate IKEA directions for the team."

Resolute
admirably purposeful, determined, and unwavering

"I have never seen anyone as *resolute* as Nia is about showcasing her cubicle Funko Pop! collection."

Indefatigable
persisting tirelessly

"Is Catalina working late again? She is *indefatigably* dedicated to helping her clients."

Tenacious

not readily relinquishing a position, principle, or course of action; determined

"I wouldn't give Adrian loose deadlines on your project. He is *tenacious* about follow-up."

Or maybe just use a simple "working hard"?

800-POUND GORILLA

A person or organization that is dominating or uncontrollable because of its great size or power. Instead, try:

Prepotent

greater than others in power or influence; how you feel after an extraordinary workout—times ten

"I am an Excel *prepotent*! Cower before my spreadsheet prowess!"

Commanding

indicating or expressing great authority

"Malik's email directives about the Homer Project deadline are *commanding*. He isn't messing around."

Unrivaled

better than everyone or everything of the same type; for example, Beyoncé

"Karen's baking is *unrivaled*. When she brings one of her layer cakes to the office, everyone flocks to the kitchen like aggressive pigeons."

RETIREMENT PARTY

ℓℓℓℓℓℓ

Some phrases feel older than time itself.
These beauts are well past their expiration date.

PEELING BACK THE ONION

To dig into the problem one layer at a time. To thoroughly understand the issue. To cry when someone utters this ancient metaphor. Instead, try:

Scrutinize
inspect closely

"I want to *scrutinize* that email chain. Something is terribly off."

Analyze
examine something methodically and in detail, typically in order to explain and interpret it

"Let's take time to *analyze* the work before we reply to that request."

Perlustrate

review and study thoroughly

"Rex decided to *perlustrate* all of the June invoices in hopes of figuring out what that new desk cost."

Ruminate

think deeply; to chew on an idea or thought; pulling a mental all-nighter

"I spent the night baking brownies and *ruminating* over ideas for the next fundraiser. And I have come up with a plan."

Excogitate

study intently and carefully in order to grasp or comprehend fully

"Did anyone *excogitate* the PowerPoint from the Swanson seminar? I am completely lost."

Suss out

to find or discover something by thinking; thinking—a dying art

"Andre is going to *suss out* the lunch thief's identity."

PREACHING TO THE CHOIR

Presenting an argument or opinion to people who already agree with it. See also: "singing from the same hymn sheet" (or hymnal) and "preaching to the converted." Instead, try:

Consensus

a general agreement among people

"It seems we have finally come to a *consensus* about using headphones in the cubes. Woohoo."

Pushing against an open door (see also: kicking at open doors)

to easily achieve victory or a desired outcome because it is supported by a majority of people

"You know, if we propose a 4 percent wage hike, we'll be *pushing against an open door* with the union."

Lecturing to the faculty

working to convince people who need no convincing

"I think reviewing the importance of sanitizing stations is *lecturing to the faculty* at this point. We're all on board."

Teaching fish how to swim

needlessly instructing people about something they already do and do well

"I'm certain I am *teaching fish how to swim* here, but HR requires me to review the timesheet process with you all."

TAKE THE BULL BY THE HORNS

To tackle a difficult task with courage and tenacity. Like quietly listening to someone use this phrase over and over without rolling your eyes. Instead, try:

Dauntless

showing fearlessness and determination

"Jada was *dauntless* in her pursuit of the perfect business trip flight—no connections, a window seat, and a cheap price."

Resolute

admirably purposeful, determined, and unwavering

"Derek held fast, *resolute* in his ability to ignore his coworker's stream of dad jokes."

Doughty

brave and persistent; envision a cross between Lassie and Wile E. Coyote

"I tell you what, Megan has been remarkably *doughty* in pursuing her promotion."

Badassery

behavior, characteristics, or actions regarded as formidably impressive

"The development team's *badassery* resulted in a 45 percent increase in donor funds this month. Ice cream party on Friday!"

PUSHING THE ENVELOPE

Extending the limits of what's possible. If you typed this phrase at any time in the past decade, you did not push the envelope. Not one bit. Instead, try:

Audacious

showing a willingness to take surprisingly bold risks

"Wow, that was one *audacious* move, Isa. I can't believe they agreed to a 150 percent increase for our rush fee."

Newfangled

a fresh idea or approach, a modern object; an old-fashioned word that's time has come again

"Loving your *newfangled* approach to this slide presentation, Zoye; really refreshing."

Radical

relating to or affecting the fundamental nature of something; far-reaching or thorough

"HR's *radical* proposal to address work from home obstacles will dramatically improve everyone's productivity. Yay, HR!"

Neoteric

a modern person; someone who advocates new ideas

"I know new ways of doing things can be intimidating, but Jason is a true *neoteric* and brings incredible ideas to the table."

Trailblazing

being the first to do something

"Prisha stepped up and took on the first trust fall. She is *trailblazing* her way through this irksome company retreat."

THINKING OUTSIDE THE BOX

If you were actually thinking outside the box, this dated and dilapidated idiom would not pass your lips. Instead, try:

Ingenious

cleverly inventive or resourceful; a MacGyver type

"Okay, that's the most *ingenious* lamp I have ever seen. It even sings!"

Offbeat

differing from the usual or expected; unconventional

"Well, it may be an *offbeat* approach, but damn if it doesn't work brilliantly."

Bellwether

a person that takes the lead or initiative, a trendsetter; like that Chicago teen who made up the term "on fleek"

"I hired Allison because she is a political polling *bellwether*."

Adroit

cleverly skillful, resourceful, or ingenious

"Creating an epic waterslide/skateboard attraction was an *adroit* solution to our theme park space dilemma."

Avant-garde

the advance group in any field, especially in the visual, literary, or musical arts, whose work is characterized chiefly by unorthodox and experimental methods

"I think our graphic designer went a bit too *avant-garde* on the client's dog toy website."

Fecund

intellectually creative or very productive

(Do note that another definition is producing or capable of producing offspring, fruit, vegetation, etc., in abundance. Just know that going into a conversation.)

"That team is so *fecund*, they developed two highly creative approaches to the problem in less than a week."

Innovatory

having the ability, curiosity, and inventiveness to create truly original stuff

"Everything about Bosco's designs is *innovatory*."

WE HAVE REACHED OUR TERMINUS

Are you full-up on obscure and yet oddly helpful work words yet? Back when you first cracked this book, a figure was thrown your way: 273,000, or the rough number of words populating the English language. Here's another number—okay, more of a range: 20,000–40,000. That is the average number of words a native English speaker knows. If you soaked this book in, you've just bridged that chasm by more than 400 words and phrases. Nice!

So, how sparkly do you feel now? Outfitted with *metagrobolize* and *donnybrook*, you may just make it happily through another tiresome conference call. Equipped with *forswunk*, *grotty*, and *borborygmus*, you could add four or five more personal days to your year. You now have the tools to write something other than "looking forward" and the email drafts to create witty autoreplies. And maybe, just maybe, you found a few choice words to help keep your coworkers' *blatherskiting* and *peenging* at bay.

Tuck this little lexicon away next to your computer and brandish it at will. You know you're going to need a creative way to ask for that deadline extension real soon. . . .

Good luck out there.

INDEX

A

B

PER MY LAST EMAIL...

Andrews McMeel Publishing
a division of Andrews McMeel Universal
1130 Walnut Street, Kansas City, Missouri 64106

www.andrewsmcmeel.com

21 22 23 24 25 VEP 10 9 8 7 6 5 4 3 2 1

ISBN: 978-1-5248-6497-2

Library of Congress Control Number: 2021937829

Editor: Allison Adler
Art Director: Tiffany Meairs
Production Editor: Amy Strassner
Production Manager: Carol Coe

ATTENTION: SCHOOLS AND BUSINESSES
Andrews McMeel books are available at quantity
discounts with bulk purchase for educational, business,
or sales promotional use. For information, please e-mail the
Andrews McMeel Publishing Special Sales Department:
specialsales@amuniversal.com.